Tommy Miah
PRESENTS

THE BEST OF
BANGLADESH

In aid of

Dhaka Orphanage Fund

KT-376-104

Tommy Miah
with
Paul Harris

First published 1987 by

Paul Harris Editorial & Publishing Consultants
Whittingehame House
Haddington
East Lothian
EH41 4QA

from whom further copies of this book can be obtained

© Copyright Tommy Miah 1987

ISBN 0 9512083 0 6

Designed by Mark Blackadder

Typesetting by Jock Westwater
and printed in Yugoslavia by Gorenjski Tisk, Kranj

Acknowledgements by the Author:

Leo Dodd Marketing Limited for their valued
assistance in this project.

British Airways Dhaka Orphanage Fund for helping
the deprived children of my home country.

Tommy Miah
P R E S E N T S

THE BEST OF
BANGLADESH

All proceeds from this book are to be
donated to the British Airways Dhaka
Orphanage Fund and will go towards the
building and running costs of a kitchen
dining area in a new home for over 400
children.

British Airways staff took the orphanage
under their wing after Stewardess Pat Kerr
highlighted the plight of the orphans who
were threatened with eviction. Building on a
new orphanage for 450 children is expected
to begin this year.

It is particularly apt that the proceeds of such
a book on the best of Bangladeshi cookery
should go to help feed underprivileged
children in that very country.

CONTENTS

TOMMY MIAH

TOMMY'S STORY

The success story of Tommy (Ajman) Miah has more than a little of the fairy tale about it. In a little over ten years, the farmer's son from Bangladesh has established two internationally renowned restaurants with a string of awards.

Tommy was born in 1959 in the village of Baronthi, Bangladesh. When Tommy was ten years old, he joined his father in Britain and enjoyed the benefit of education at Junior School and then Secondary School in Birmingham.

When he was 16 he left school and returned briefly to his home to marry a local girl, Rina, from the same district, but very quickly he was back in Birmingham where his ambition and industry was soon apparent. He studied hard the art of Asian Cuisine and soon became Head Chef in one of Birmingham's most prominent Indian restaurants.

Tommy had always wanted his own restaurant. The only way was to step out of the security of his job as Head Chef and open an Asian 'Carry-Out'. With Rina's help day and night, the 'Carry-Out' paved the way for Tommy to realise his life long ambition—his own restaurant.

The market in both Birmingham and London was well supplied with Asian restaurants and it was to Edinburgh that Tommy looked. "There was room for a new type of Indian restaurant away from the traditional dark and unimaginative designs."

After looking around Edinburgh, Tommy decided that the up and coming area was Leith and with the encouragement of the SDA (Scottish Development Agency), he acquired one of the best sites in the area at the corner of Henderson Street. Formerly a warehouse and a snooker hall, in earlier history the building was the Empire Cinema House which had opened its doors on April 14th 1913 at the height of the popularity of the silent film. It is recorded that the first night audience found the hall of the cinema graced with potted palms when they took their seats for a showing of *A Tale of Two Cities*. The cinema seated 600 patrons and enjoyed great popularity until the arrival of the 'talkies' and it was forced to close in 1930.

This graceful old building, with its panoramic views down the Water of Leith, was absolutely ideal for Tommy's plans and *The Raj* was born —a restaurant with a truly unique atmosphere *The Raj* was quickly welcomed by the professional food critics and dining public alike. There were write-ups in *The Observer, The Scotsman* and, even, a newspaper in Washington D.C.! In December 1986 *The Raj* secured the top Asian food nomination from *The Scotsman* when it was nominated Indian Restaurant of The Year.

A vital feature of any restaurant run by Tommy is his own presence at the front of the restaurant organising things, chatting with the customers and generally impressing his personality on the establishment. Tommy feels this personal touch is all important although it leaves him with a very tight schedule to fit in his interests in a successful property company, his family and his other great love—football.

For Tommy, his family life is of paramount importance and he spends as much time as he can with his 9 year-old daughter Aysha, 8 year-old son Rajah and his recently born son Rajoo. "Edinburgh was a good move for me. It is an excellent place to bring up a family. I have never found any prejudice and so many people here have helped me with my business. I am very happy here but I sometimes feel a little homesick for my relatives at home." Football is very popular in Bangladesh and when he lived in Birmingham young Tommy played at every opportunity. He is now both a supporter and sponsor of *Meadowbank Thistle*.

And then, of course there is his favourite hobby —cooking—which this book is all about. For the future, there will be other restaurants with a new one already in Edinburgh's Forrest Road —Miah's. Each one will be individual and special and Tommy intends to retain that personal control and contact with his customers.

Meantime, he is happy to share some of his culinary secrets with all his many friends and diners, old and new. Moreover Tommy is donating all the money from sales of this book to the *British Airways Dhaka Orphanage Fund* as a gesture of his profound appreciation of the endless efforts being made by Pat Kerr and her team in helping the underpriviledged children of his homeland.

ONCE RARE AND EXOTIC, ALL THESE SPICES ARE NOW
WIDELY AVAILABLE

A NOTE FROM THE CHEF

All these recipes are really quite simple and are suitable for preparation by the most unsophisticated cook in an ordinary kitchen. I have tried to make the instructions very simple and they are all presented as a simple step-by-step operation.

If any help is required in obtaining ingredients please refer to the back of this book. You should be able to obtain easily any ingredients specified here.

All the recipes will serve approximately four people—depending on appetite!

All spoon measurements are level. Both Imperial and Metric measurements are given. All eggs are standard sizes. Remember to preheat the oven or grill to the required temperature.

Do grind your spices freshly—this will make an enormous difference. It is not difficult and produces an enormously more flavoursome dish than packaged curry powders. Dry spices in their whole form will remain fresh for quite long periods if stored in cool, dry and dark places in tightly lidded jars. Then just grind your spices as you need them using an electric grinder or the more old fashioned mortar and pestle will do the job perfectly adequately.

If you follow these few simple instructions there is no reason why you cannot quickly enjoy the Best of Bangladesh.

Happy Cooking!

Tommy Miah

Pakora with Imli Sauce

A popular starter served with a sauce made from juice of the tamarind.

1 Mix the ingredients for the batter to produce a smooth paste.

2 After slicing, wash the vegetables and dry in a teacloth.

3 Heat the oil in a saucepan until hot.

4 Dip the slices of vegetables in your batter and put in the hot oil. Fry until crisp and golden. Remove from the oil with a slotted spoon, drain and serve with Imli sauce.

To prepare the Imli Sauce

5 The tamarind should be soaked in water for around 30 minutes.

6 Squeeze the pulp and draw out all the juice you can.

7 Chop two onions. Fry in ghee or oil. Salt to taste. Add 1 fresh tomato (chopped) and 2 fresh green chillis (or more, depending on how hot you like it). Sweeten with sugar.

8 Add Imli juice. Boil together. Thin with a cup of water as necessary and add red colouring before serving. You will now have a delicious hot, sweet and sour sauce.

BATTER

4 tbsp flour

2 tsp oil

1 tsp baking powder

½ tsp salt

3 fl oz/75 ml water

½ tsp turmeric
Leaves of fresh corriander or parsley to taste

VEGETABLES

Select according to taste: aubergine: cut into thin rounds onion: cut into rings, potato: cut into thin rounds, cauliflower: cut into small florets, etc.

Use one vegetable or mix various

Oil for deep frying

IMLI SAUCE

3 oz/75 g dried tamarind

8 fl oz/225 ml hot water

2 onions

Ghee or oil

Salt

1 fresh tomato

2 fresh green chillies (to taste)

2 tsp sugar

Chilli powder to taste

Seekh Kebabs

Delicious kebabs grilled on skewers

1 Slice lemon; remove pips.
2 Slice onion rings.
3 Skin and slice tomato.
4 Mix the egg and mince in a bowl, adding baisn.
5 Add spices, salt and the juice from the lemon.
6 Fold meat around skewers (it may be easier if you rub some butter or ghee on your fingers); baste with cooking fat and grill gently, turning so the meat is cooked evenly.
7 Slide kebabs off skewers and serve as a starter; garnish with lemon slices, onion rings and tomato slices.

½ lb/500 g lamb (finely minced)
1 lemon
1 onion
1 tomato
1 large egg
2 tbsp baisn
1 tsp coriander (ground)
½ tsp cumin (ground)
½ tsp chilli powder
½ tsp garam masala
Salt to taste
Ghee or oil

STARTERS: PAKORA, SEEKH KEBABS, SAMOSAS AND FISH
KEBABS

Samosas

Tasty meat-stuffed pastries served as a starter.

1 Prepare your pastry first, sifting flour, salt and baking powder, rub in ghee. Make dough (soft) by adding water.

2 Prepare filling, first heating ghee or oil in a saucepan and frying onion. Add a little water and fry mince gently for 10 minutes, stirring occasionally. Add green chilli, coriander and lemon juice. Mix well. Allow to cool.

3 Knead dough well and divide into approximately 1½ doz. balls. Use a little flour and roll out balls into 4" (10 cm) rounds; cut across centre, add flour paste down straight edge and bring the two corners together to make a cone, pressing pasted edges together to secure.

4 Insert filling into cone; apply flour paste to the open mouth and seal the shape.

5 Take a deep frying pan and heat the oil. Deep fry samosas until golden brown; remove with slotted spoon, draining. You can serve hot or cold with a branded sauce or Imli sauce.

6 You can serve hot or cold with a branded sauce or Imli sauce.

PASTRY

5 oz/150 g plain flour

Pinch of salt

¼ tsp baking powder

Ghee or oil

Water to mix

FILLING

8 oz/225 g lean mince

½ oz/15 g ghee or 1 tbsp oil

1 onion, peeled and chopped

4 oz/112 g garden peas

Salt

Freshly ground black pepper

1 green chilli, finely chopped

2/3 sprigs fresh coriander leaves, chopped

Juice of ½ lemon

FLOUR PASTE

2/3 tsp plain flour mixed with a little water

Oil for deep frying

Bengali Fish Kebabs

A traditional dish from my homeland which makes a delicious starter.

1 Cut the fish into cubes.
2 Grind the garlic and add to the water in which fish is to be washed.
3 Wash and drain fish cubes.
4 Slice chillis, grind onions and mix with yoghurt, salt and spices.
5 Marinate fish in this mixture for 2 hours.
6 Drain and dry.
7 Thread fish on to skewers and grill, moistening with melted butter.
8 Serve on a bed of salad.

Ingredients
2 lb/1 kg firm-fleshed fish
2 cloves garlic
2 onions
6 fl oz/150 ml yoghurt
Salt to taste
½ tsp ginger
1 tsp turmeric powder
2 tsp garam masala
1 fresh green chilli
Chilli powder to taste
Melted butter for basting

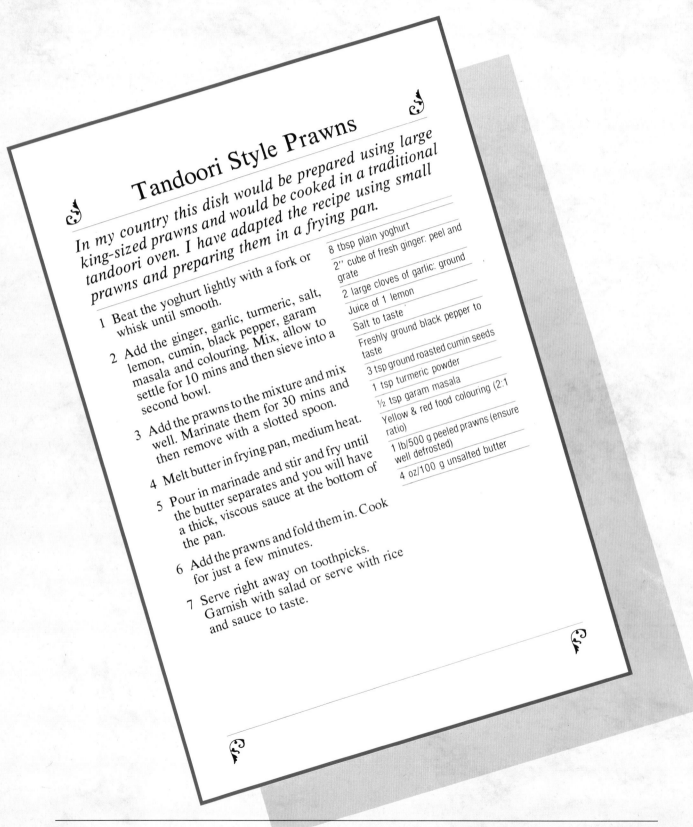

Tandoori Style Prawns

In my country this dish would be prepared using large king-sized prawns and would be cooked in a traditional tandoori oven. I have adapted the recipe using small prawns and preparing them in a frying pan.

1 Beat the yoghurt lightly with a fork or whisk until smooth.

2 Add the ginger, garlic, turmeric, salt, lemon, cumin, black pepper, garam masala and colouring. Mix, allow to settle for 10 mins and then sieve into a second bowl.

3 Add the prawns to the mixture and mix well. Marinate them for 30 mins and then remove with a slotted spoon.

4 Melt butter in frying pan, medium heat.

5 Pour in marinade and stir and fry until the butter separates and you will have a thick, viscous sauce at the bottom of the pan.

6 Add the prawns and fold them in. Cook for just a few minutes.

7 Serve right away on toothpicks. Garnish with salad or serve with rice and sauce to taste.

8 tbsp plain yoghurt

2" cube of fresh ginger: peel and grate

2 large cloves of garlic: ground

Juice of 1 lemon

Salt to taste

Freshly ground black pepper to taste

3 tsp ground roasted cumin seeds

1 tsp turmeric powder

½ tsp garam masala

Yellow & red food colouring (2:1 ratio)

1 lb/500 g peeled prawns (ensure well defrosted)

4 oz/100 g unsalted butter

TANDOORI STYLE PRAWNS GARNISHED WITH SALAD

TANDOORI MURGH

Tandoori Murgh

In Bangladesh Tandoori chicken is traditionally cooked in the special oven known as a 'Tandoor'. These are now available from specialist kitchen shops and stores like Habitat but if you do not have one this dish can be cooked in the oven or on a rotary spit.

1 Clean chicken and make 3 or 4 cuts on each side of the bird.

2 Grind onion and garlic to a paste and then add cumin, chilli, coriander, ginger and salt.

3 Lightly beat the yoghurt in a bowl and add the paste, vinegar and juice of 1 lemon. Mix well and rub on chicken.

4 Marinate chicken for at least 8 hours and, if possible, for 24/48 hours in the refrigerator.

5 Roast chicken in a moderate oven until tender (about 1 hour) basting with the marinade and ghee.

6 Brush with melted butter, sprinkle on garam masala and lemon juice and serve with breads and salad.

Ingredients
1 2lb/1 kg roasting chicken
1 onion
4 cloves garlic
½ tsp ginger (ground)
1 tsp coriander (ground)
½ tsp chilli powder
2 tsp salt
6 fl oz/150 ml yoghurt
1 tbsp vinegar
2 lemons
Melted butter for basting
Garam masala for garnishing

VEGETARIAN

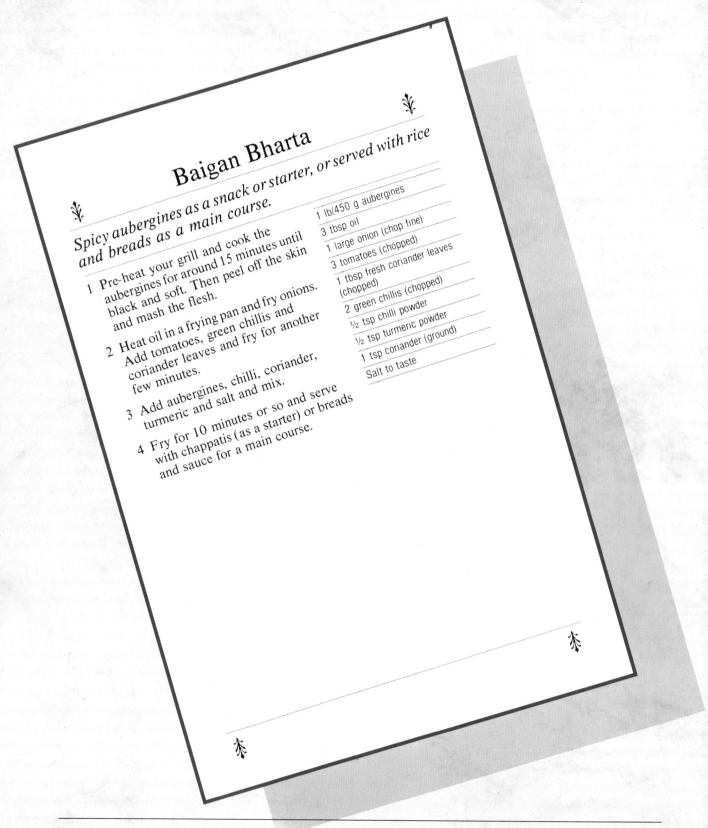

Baigan Bharta

Spicy aubergines as a snack or starter, or served with rice and breads as a main course.

1 Pre-heat your grill and cook the aubergines for around 15 minutes until black and soft. Then peel off the skin and mash the flesh.

2 Heat oil in a frying pan and fry onions. Add tomatoes, green chillis and coriander leaves and fry for another few minutes.

3 Add aubergines, chilli, coriander, turmeric and salt and mix.

4 Fry for 10 minutes or so and serve with chappatis (as a starter) or breads and sauce for a main course.

Ingredients
1 lb/450 g aubergines
3 tbsp oil
1 large onion (chop fine)
3 tomatoes (chopped)
1 tbsp fresh coriander leaves (chopped)
2 green chillis (chopped)
½ tsp chilli powder
½ tsp turmeric powder
1 tsp coriander (ground)
Salt to taste

Aloo Zeera

This dry spiced potato curry is characterised by the aromatic taste of cumin.

1 Take a heavy frying pan and dry roast the cumin and fenugreek for 1 minute.

2 Add the chopped onion, chopped chillis and half the oil or ghee and fry for 1 further minute.

3 Grind the mixture with a little water to form a fine paste.

4 Heat remaining oil or ghee in a pan and add the bay leaves and mustard seeds. Fry for ½ minute, then add paste, the cooked potatoes, turmeric and salt to taste.

5 Add a little water, cover on pan and cook on a medium heat for 3 minutes or so.

Ingredients
2 tsp whole cumin seeds
½ tsp fenugreek seeds
2 fresh red chillis
1 onion, peeled & chopped
2 tbsp oil or ghee
½ doz. bay leaves
1 tsp mustard seeds
1 lb/500 g new potatoes (if possible), boiled, peeled and cut small
Salt to taste
½ tsp turmeric powder

VEGETARIAN DISHES: ALOO ZEERA, EGG CURRY, BAIGAN
BARTA AND VEGETARIAN CURRY

Vegetable Curry

More and more people these days prefer vegetarian dishes and this is an easy recipe for a vegetable curry which can be prepared in 20 minutes or so.

1 In a saucepan fry the onion, garlic, curry powder and turmeric in the oil or ghee.

2 Mix in the tomatoes, chillis and coriander and add water as necessary to make a gravy.

3 Add the vegetables and salt to taste.

4 Simmer for around 20 minutes until the vegetables are cooked.

5 Squeeze in some lemon juice to taste.

6 Serve with rice or breads.

Ingredients
1 lb/500 g fresh vegetables (e.g. peas, carrots, beans, cauliflower and potatoes)
2 tbsp ghee or oil
1 onion (sliced)
2 green chillis (quartered)
2 cloves garlic (sliced)
½ lb/250 g tomatoes (chopped)
2 tbsp Madras curry powder
1 tsp turmeric powder
Salt to taste
Water
Fresh lemon juice to taste

Egg Curry

Eggs are not extensively used in any Indian cookery but they can be used to make a cheap and tasty dish which is very easy to prepare.

1 Heat the ghee or oil in a pan over a medium heat. Gently fry the onions.

2 Add the cinnamon stick and stir. Stir in chilli powder, garlic, ginger, coriander, cumin and garam masala. Fry gently for ½ minute or so.

3 Add the tomatoes and salt. Fry for 5 minutes: the mixture will thicken. Stir in the water and add the eggs.

4 Cover pan and allow to simmer gently for about 10 minutes.

5 Garnish with coriander or parsley and serve with a bread.

Ingredients
8 hard boiled eggs (shelled)
2 onions (peeled and chopped)
1 1"/2.5 cm stick cinnamon
1 tsp garlic powder
1 tsp ginger (ground)
1 tsp chilli powder
1 tsp cumin (ground)
1½ tsp coriander (ground)
1 tsp garam masala
1 8 oz/225 g can of tomatoes (chopped)
½ pint/300 ml water
Salt to taste
Ghee or oil

Bangladeshi Fish Kofta

A most popular dish from my homeland.

1 Cook the fish until it is tender in 2/3 cups of water together with half a chopped onion, salt and a bay leave.	2 lbs/1 kg white fish
	3 onions
2 Remove with slotted spoon; retain liquid.	1 bay leaf
	Salt
3 Chop green chillis and coriander leaves.	2 green chillis
	3/4 sprigs fresh coriander
4 Mash fish and mix with chopped chillis, coriander leaves, the egg and baisn (gram flour).	1 egg
	2 tbsp baisn or gram flour
	1 clove garlic
5 Shape into small balls and fry in ghee or oil until brown. Remove from pan with slotted spoon.	1 tsp coriander (ground)
	½ tsp cumin (ground)
	1 tsp turmeric powder
6 Slice one onion finely.	1 tsp chilli powder
	Ghee or vegetable oil

7 Grind balance of the onions and garlic into a paste and add the other spices.

8 Heat ghee or oil and fry sliced onion until golden brown. Add chopped tomatoes and salt and cook with cover on pan for 5 minutes, stirring occasionally.

9 Add the liquid from the preparation of the fish and cook liquid, fish balls and spice mixture all together on a medium heat for 10 minutes.

10 Serve with rice or breads.

BANGLADESHI FISH KOFTA AND FISH IN A BANGLADESHI
SAUCE

Chingree in Coconut

In this traditional dish prawns are served in a rich, hot sauce on a bed of plain rice. If you prefer it milder do not add the chilli powder. In Britain small prawns would be easiest to obtain and I have used them for this recipe. In Bangladesh we would use the giant prawns (illustrated) which are plentiful and which I fly in to my restaurants.

1 Ensure prawns are washed; pat dry.

2 Heat small frying pan over medium heat and put in coriander seeds, peppercorns and fenugreek seeds. Lightly roast, stirring, for 1 minute.

3 Put in grinder together with curry leaves, grind fine.

4 Heat oil in standard frying pan and put in mustard seeds. When they pop add onion and garlic. Stir and fry. Add the ginger. Stir. Add 1½ cups water, paprika, chilli powder (optional), turmeric, salt, whole chillis, ground spice mixture and lemon juice.

5 Bring to the boil and then simmer for 5 minutes. Your sauce is now ready. You can either keep it or proceed.

6 Put in the prawns and stir for 3/4 minutes. Pour in coconut milk and stir vigorously. As soon as contents of the pan start to boil, serve with plain rice.

Ingredients
1 lb/500 g peeled prawns (defrost well if frozen)
1 tbs coriander seeds
¼ tsp fenugreek seeds
1 tsp black peppercorns
6 dried curry leaves
2 tsp lemon juice
1 tsp black mustard seeds
1 onion (peeled and cut into rings)
4 cloves garlic (peeled and cut fine)
1 tsp fresh ginger (peeled and finely grated)
1 tbs red paprika
1 tsp chilli powder
½ tsp turmeric powder
Salt
3 fresh green chillis
1½ cups tinned coconut milk (unsweetened) or use creamed coconut
Vegetable oil

CHINGREE IN COCONUT

Fish in a Bangladeshi Sauce

This is an immensely popular dish at home where fish are plentiful and consumed regularly. It would normally be served with plain rice.

1 Rub fish with mixture of salt and turmeric (½ tsp each). Set aside for 15 minutes.

2 Heat oil in frying pan and brown fish pieces lightly. Lift out fish with slotted spoon.

3 Mix ground coriander seeds, ginger, cumin, chilli powder, turmeric and salt, adding 3 tbs of water.

4 Remove most of oil from frying pan and heat about 5 tbsp over medium heat. Put in red chillis, then bay leaves. As they darken add onion and fry until golden brown.

5 Add spice mixture. Stir and fry for 1 minute.

6 Add fish pieces and a cup of water, spread pieces around bottom of pan and lay green chillis on top. Simmer for a couple of minutes covering with sauce.

7 Cover pan and let cook on low heat for about 15 minutes until fish is done.

8 Serve with plain rice.

1½ lb/600 g haddock, cod or any other white fish cubed in 1½/2" pieces

½ tsp ground turmeric

Salt

Vegetable oil

1 tsp cumin

1 tbsp coriander

1½ tsp ginger (finely grated, fresh)

½ tsp chilli powder

4 whole red chillis

2 bay leaves

1 large onion (peeled and chopped)

3 green chillis (whole)

1 tsp turmeric powder

MEAT

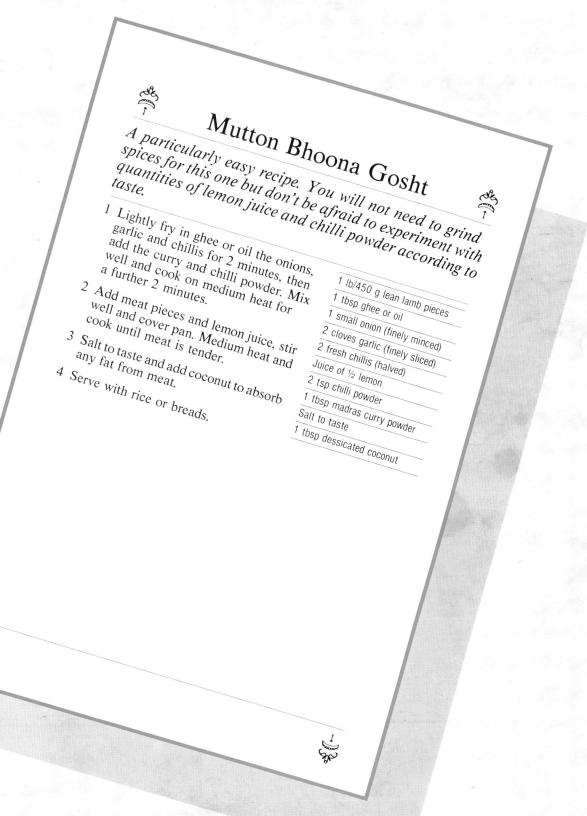

Mutton Bhoona Gosht

A particularly easy recipe. You will not need to grind spices for this one but don't be afraid to experiment with quantities of lemon juice and chilli powder according to taste.

1 Lightly fry in ghee or oil the onions, garlic and chillis for 2 minutes, then add the curry and chilli powder. Mix well and cook on medium heat for a further 2 minutes.

2 Add meat pieces and lemon juice, stir well and cover pan. Medium heat and cook until meat is tender.

3 Salt to taste and add coconut to absorb any fat from meat.

4 Serve with rice or breads.

Ingredients
1 lb/450 g lean lamb pieces
1 tbsp ghee or oil
1 small onion (finely minced)
2 cloves garlic (finely sliced)
2 fresh chillis (halved)
Juice of ½ lemon
2 tsp chilli powder
1 tbsp madras curry powder
Salt to taste
1 tbsp dessicated coconut

Lamb Passanda

This is a most popular dish which few people have probably tried at home. It is not difficult if you follow these instructions and you should be able to prepare successfully this characteristically rich, creamy and mild dish.

1 Mix together in large bowl the meat, yoghurt, garlic, ginger, coriander, cumin, almonds, garam masala and salt. Cover and let marinate for 2 hours.

2 Heat ghee in frying pan, add onion and cook until golden brown.

3 Add meat and spice mixture; fry until meat is browned.

4 Cover and cook for 30 minutes or so, adding milk, bay leaves, cardamom pods and cinnamon stick.

5 Add yoghurt and/or double cream according to taste for consistency.

6 Garnish with coriander leaves and almonds and serve with rice or breads.

1 lb/500 g lean lamb, cut into thin pieces

¼ pint/150 ml natural yoghurt

3 garlic cloves, peeled and crushed

1 oz/25 g fresh ginger (peeled and crushed

1 tsp coriander (ground)

1½ tsp cumin (ground)

½ oz /13 g almonds (ground)

1 tsp garam masala powder

2 bay leaves

5 cardamom pods

1 cinnamon stick

Salt

Ghee or vegetable oil

1 onion (finely chopped)

Water

1 cup milk

Yoghurt or double cream for consistency

Garnishing—
Chopped coriander leaves
Flaked almonds

LAMB PASSANDA GARNISHED WITH CORIANDER AND
OKRA AND SERVED WITH CHAPATIS

MUTTON BHOONA GOSHT AND MUTTON ROGAN JOSH
WITH POPPADUMS

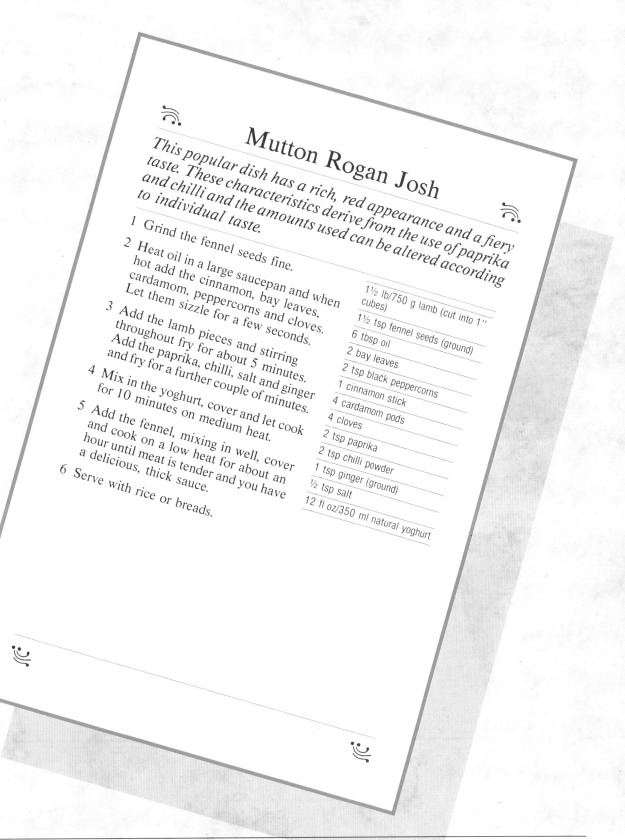

Mutton Rogan Josh

This popular dish has a rich, red appearance and a fiery taste. These characteristics derive from the use of paprika and chilli and the amounts used can be altered according to individual taste.

1 Grind the fennel seeds fine.

2 Heat oil in a large saucepan and when hot add the cinnamon, bay leaves, cardamom, peppercorns and cloves. Let them sizzle for a few seconds.

3 Add the lamb pieces and stirring throughout fry for about 5 minutes. Add the paprika, chilli, salt and ginger and fry for a further couple of minutes.

4 Mix in the yoghurt, cover and let cook for 10 minutes on medium heat.

5 Add the fennel, mixing in well, cover and cook on a low heat for about an hour until meat is tender and you have a delicious, thick sauce.

6 Serve with rice or breads.

Ingredients
1½ lb/750 g lamb (cut into 1" cubes)
1½ tsp fennel seeds (ground)
6 tbsp oil
2 bay leaves
2 tsp black peppercorns
1 cinnamon stick
4 cardamom pods
4 cloves
2 tsp paprika
2 tsp chilli powder
1 tsp ginger (ground)
½ tsp salt
12 fl oz/350 ml natural yoghurt

Keema with Garden Peas

Mince must be one of the most popular everyday dishes. This recipe for a dry mince curry is a simple way of putting some spice into your mince.

1 Heat the oil or ghee over a medium heat in a large pan. Fry onion lightly. Add cinnamon stick, bay leaf and cardamoms. Fry for 1 minute.

2 Add your minced beef or lamb. Sprinkle on the turmeric, cumin, coriander and chilli powder, mixing in well.

3 Fry until meat is browned then add the yoghurt and salt. Cover pan and cook for 10/15 minutes by which time the mince will be dry.

4 Add peas and cook gently for a further 10 minutes.

5 Serve with bread such as pitta or parathas.

1 lb/500 g minced lamb or beef
1 onion (peeled and chopped)
1 1"/2.5 cm cinnamon stick
6 cardamoms (whole)
1 bay leaf
½ tsp turmeric powder
1 tsp chilli powder
1 tsp coriander (ground)
2 tsp cumin (ground)
¼ pint/150 ml natural yoghurt
4 oz/100 g peas (fresh or frozen)
Ghee or vegetable oil

KEEMA WITH GARDEN PEAS

MURGH DO PIAZA GARNISHED WITH CORIANDER AND
SERVED WITH CURRY SAUCE

CHICKEN

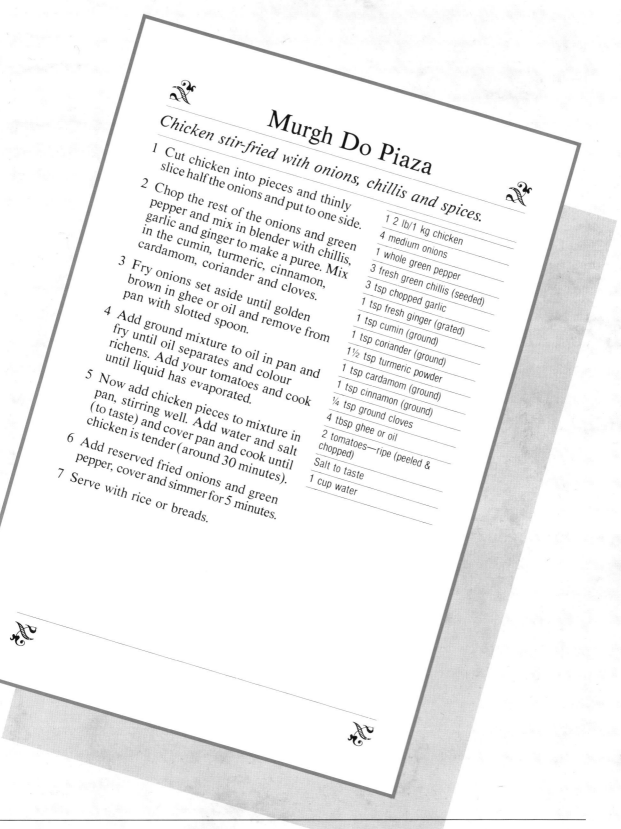

Murgh Do Piaza

Chicken stir-fried with onions, chillis and spices.

1 Cut chicken into pieces and thinly slice half the onions and put to one side.

2 Chop the rest of the onions and green pepper and mix in blender with chillis, garlic and ginger to make a puree. Mix in the cumin, turmeric, cinnamon, cardamom, coriander and cloves.

3 Fry onions set aside until golden brown in ghee or oil and remove from pan with slotted spoon.

4 Add ground mixture to oil in pan and fry until oil separates and colour richens. Add your tomatoes and cook until liquid has evaporated.

5 Now add chicken pieces to mixture in pan, stirring well. Add water and salt (to taste) and cover pan and cook until chicken is tender (around 30 minutes).

6 Add reserved fried onions and green pepper, cover and simmer for 5 minutes.

7 Serve with rice or breads.

Ingredients
1 2 lb/1 kg chicken
4 medium onions
1 whole green pepper
3 fresh green chillis (seeded)
3 tsp chopped garlic
1 tsp fresh ginger (grated)
1 tsp cumin (ground)
1 tsp coriander (ground)
1½ tsp turmeric powder
1 tsp cardamom (ground)
1 tsp cinnamon (ground)
¼ tsp ground cloves
4 tbsp ghee or oil
2 tomatoes—ripe (peeled & chopped)
Salt to taste
1 cup water

MURGH MASALLAM WITH BASMATI RICE

Murgh Masallam

A most popular spicy roast chicken dish.

1. Slice onions finely.
2. Grind garlic, cardamoms and cumin seeds, to a paste. Add the other spices to the paste and water and salt as necessary.
3. Rub your trussed and cleaned chicken with the paste.
4. Heat ghee or oil in a pan and fry onions gently until golden brown; remove and put aside.
5. Put chicken in the pan with the rest of the marsala paste and fry.
6. Beat yoghurt until smooth and add fried onions. Pour over chicken and bring to the boil, then allow to simmer until chicken is tender (about 45 mins.)
7. Uncover and fry until excess liquid is absorbed.
8. Serve chicken on a platter with a sauce separately in a bowl.

1 3 lb/1½ kg chicken, cleaned
3 large onions
4 cloves garlic
2 black cardamoms, large
½ tsp cumin seeds
Salt to taste
Ghee or oil
12 fl oz/450 ml yoghurt
MARSALA PASTE
2 tsp cumin
1 tsp turmeric powder
1 tsp chilli powder
¼ tsp clove powder
1 tsp cinnamon
1 tsp ginger
½ tsp black pepper (freshly ground)

Murgh Jahl Frezie

Chicken with onions and vegetables — a fast, tasty dish.

1 Chop finely two of the onions and slice the other; place to one side.

2 Grind garlic and ginger.

3 Heat oil in a large frying pan and fry the chopped onions and spice mixture until onions are golden.

4 Add chicken, sliced onions, green chillis, turmeric, chilli powder, salt and vegetables and fry for about 10 minutes until the vegetables are tender.

5 Add the yoghurt and tomato and fry for a couple of minutes.

6 Serve with breads or rice.

Ingredients
1 lb/450 g chicken pieces (small)
3 medium onions
3 tbsp oil
2 cloves garlic (ground)
½"/1 cm ginger (ground)
4 green chillis, chopped
½ tsp turmeric powder
½ tsp chilli powder
4 oz/100 g fresh mixed vegetables
Salt to taste
3 fl oz/150 ml yoghurt
1 tomato, peeled and cut

MURGH JAHL FREZIE

RICE AND BREADS

I recommend that you try to perfect just two types of rice: basmati and plain, or long grain, rice.

The best basmati rice is aged before it is sold—sometimes for up to a year and it has a delightful fragrance. Before you cook it, though, you should pick it over, wash and then soak for around half an hour. After soaking, drain in a sieve for another twenty minutes or so to the point where it is almost dry before you cook it. You will then find that your rice will need less water to cook, it will come out light and separated and will be far more pleasant to actually eat.

Also when cooking rice use the heaviest pot you have and make sure it has a tight lid. Do not allow the steam to escape. Get rid of all the starch you can in the washing process (this is left over from the milling and is not required). Never use more than 1½ parts liquid to 1 part rice in cooking and cook on a very low heat. Remove rice from pot using a slotted spoon. You will remember that I have used this implement in other recipes here and a large one is essential in the kitchen.

Plain Long Grain Rice

1 Wash rice in several changes of water and drain.

2 Soak in 2 pints (1½ litres) of water for 30 mins. Then drain thoroughly.

3 Put drained rice, salt and water in heavy pot and bring to boil. Cover with tight fitting lid and cook on a low heat for about half an hour.

4 Remove rice pot from the heat and leave it uncovered for 10 minutes before serving— use slotted spoon.

Long grain rice (fill measuring jug to 15 fl oz/425 ml level)

1 tsp salt

1 pt/570 ml water

Basmati Rice

1 Pick over rice and place in a bowl.

2 Wash thoroughly changing water several times. Drain.

Basmati rice (fill measuring jug to 15 fl oz/425 ml level)

1 tsp salt

½ oz/10 g unsalted butter

1 pt/570 ml water

3 Soak in 2 pints/1½ litres water for half and hour. Drain thoroughly.

4 Rice, salt, butter and water in a heavy pot and bring to boil. Cover with a tight fitting lid and cook on a low heat for about half and hour.

4 Lift lid and mix quickly with a fork and cover again. Cook for another 5 minutes or so until soft.

We eat many different types of breads and to me they are an essential part of any meal. The chappati is very popular and is a piece of dough rolled out into a circular shape about 8 in. in diameter which is placed on a hot griddle where it is cooked without oil or ghee.

The paratha is thicker than the chappati although about the same size. It is prepared by shallow frying in oil but should remain crisp on the surface when removed from the oil. It can be served plain or stuffed with meat or vegetables.

Chappatis

1 Sift flour and salt together and gradually add water to make a soft dough. Knead well.

2 Shape the dough into small balls. On a floured base roll out each ball into a round approx. 7 in. in diameter.

3 Gently heat up your griddle or a heavy frying pan and place a round of dough in it. When it starts to brown turn it over and cook on other side. Do not allow to harden.

4 Brush melted ghee or butter on the top and wrap in a tea towel to keep soft before serving.

1 lb/450 g plain wholemeal flour

Pinch of salt

4 fl oz/120 ml water

Melted ghee or butter

Parathas

1 Mix flour and salt together and gradually add water to make a soft dough. Knead well and divide into around 15 portions.

2 On a floured base roll out into round, square or other shapes. Brush ghee or butter over surface. Fold in half and repeat the operation. You will now have a small triangle which should be rolled out thinly with a little more flour.

3 Gently heat up a heavy frying pan and cook on each side for 1/2 minutes. Brush with melted ghee or oil again and gently fry until golden brown. Do not allow to harden.

4 Brush ghee or butter on top and wrap in tea towel to keep soft before serving.

1 lb/450 g plain wholemeal flour

Pinch of salt

4 fl oz/120 ml water

Melted ghee or oil

GLOSSARY
OF TERMS USED

Aloo Potato

Baigan Aubergines

Baisn Fine flour, slightly yellow in colour

Bhaji Vegetables cooked so as to absorb heat of chillis and spices

Bhindi Lady's fingers (okra)

Bhoona Gosht Dry curry in which spiced meat is fried in spices

Biryani Rice cooked with curry sauce and meat, usually garnished

Chappati Wholewheat unleavened griddle bread

Chingree Prawn

Chitchkee Vegetable curry

Do Piaza Meat or chicken stir-fried with onions, spices and chillies and simmered until tender

Garam Masala Powder of ground cardamoms, cloves, cumin, coriander seeds and peppercorns

Ghee Clarified butter

Jahl Chicken or meat stir-fried in onion, garlic, chilli, ginger and other spices

Kebabs Pieces of meat or fish cooked in their own juices or skewered and grilled or minced and made into cutlets and then fried: **seekh** mutton pieces minced, mixed with spices and grilled

Keema Minced beef or lamb cooked with onions, spices and chillis

Kofta Balls of minced meat or fish blended with onions, spices, etc. and cooked in a curry sauce

Murgh Chicken

Naan Baked leavened bread

Nareal Coconut

Pakoras Spiced fritters with fresh vegetables

Paratha Griddle-fried bread made with ghee often stuffed with meat or vegetables

Parotha Chappatis rolled together to make a multi-layered bread

Passanda Meat slices marinated, fried and simmered until tender and served after addition of yoghurt and cream

Rogan Josh Lamb pieces marinated and cooked with spices until tender, usually hot and fiery

Samosa Flour dough shells stuffed with mince meat and/or vegetables cooked in spices and onion

Tandoori Special charcoal fired brick or clay oven in which poultry, meat or fish can be cooked to impart a delicious flavour

Tandoori Murgh Chicken pieces marinated and then roasted in tandoori oven

Tarka dal Lentils cooked in a spicy broth

Yoghurt Common ingredient and food in Asian cuisine as a side dish, marinade base and to impart consistency and flavour to main dishes